TRUSTING GOD

THE PATH OF LEAST RESISTANCE

SHILPA GOEL

Made with ♥ on the Notion Press Platform
www.notionpress.com

This book is dedicated to God who sent me this idea and wrote this book through me. It is also dedicated to my daughter Ashvika, whom I carried in me while this book was being born.

।।जय माता दी।।

Contents

Preface

February 27, 2022

I don't know why but I felt called to write this book this morning.

I was sitting and praying after getting ready in the morning, the way I do every day. And one after the other thoughts came to my mind, leading me to this: Trusting God, the path of least resistance.

The title came to me as if gods themselves spoke from their respective images.

I could not wait to note it down in my list of ideas for the fear of forgetting it.

But you know what? When things are meant for you, they don't leave you until you have received them or done them.

It's afternoon now and words came to me for this introduction, nagging me to note them down and start writing this book already.

It's raw. I won't edit it much. I will also try to keep it short.

If I am meant to write this book, maybe you are meant to read this, too.

See, I am really good at procrastinating. I wasn't expecting to start writing this book for another couple of months, let alone on the same day.

And I have put an urgent work aside just so that I can draft this introduction as words are somehow being poured into my mind by, I guess, God.

Now, this is what I call the path of least resistance.

My second poetry book is almost done, except for a round of editing, but I am too resistant in sending out its proposal to publishers.

My other e-book's outline is ready but I am too resistant in starting to write it.

My novel, which I began in 2019, is stuck on its ending. I drafted the plot and lost it. But I know the ending. I am just resistant about working on it.

I still don't know if I would publish this book any sooner but as far as writing this introduction is concerned, I let God write through me. I trust God. I choose the path of the least resistance.

This book may be full of imperfections and flaws because, for once, I am putting my fear of perfection aside and letting God guide this book and channelise His message through me.

It's okay if you don't believe in God. Maybe you believe in the Universe, in your Higher Self, in your Creator, or any name that you have given to a power greater than all else, it's all same. Trust whichever higher power you believe in.

Acknowledgements

No book of mine ever comes into existence without God. This one, I believe, is a work of God. So, how can it be complete without thanking God first? I thank God for this book and for everything in my life.

Thanks to my parents for taking me closer to God and giving me the lessons that have saved my life, for the way they raised me, and for always standing by my side.

Thanks to my husband, parents-in-law, brother, and sisters-in-law for being a constant support and for being so loving and caring.

Thanks to my friends who have been with me on my writing journey since the beginning and for supporting me incessantly.

Every book finds its destination in the hands of a reader. Thanks to you all for picking this or any of my books and providing them with their destination. You all make the efforts that go into a book worth it.

The PDF version of this book is available on Gumroad. I wrote this book and launched the e-Book when I was 5 months pregnant with my daughter Ashvika. She's sitting in my lap as I am formatting the paperback version. She let me write this book peacefully when she was in, she's letting me format it peacefully when she's out. I'm truly blessed to have her.

I

What Does Trusting God Look Like?

Trusting God, it's easier said than done, but to be honest, there is just one requirement, one ingredient, one step that is needed to trust God and we call it FAITH.

I am not even saying unwavering faith.

We make trusting God seem harder than it is. We feel like we need to try hard in order to have unwavering faith in the Almighty.

It's okay if your faith wavers. It happens even to the most devoted human beings. And God forgives. God knows we are humans, we are bound to drift off on alternate paths at times. God made us humans and as Alexander Pope said, "to err is human."

What matters is that you find the path of faith again and again and even again every time you find yourself drifting away from that path.

So, it's okay if people, situations, and emotions make your faith waver. Just remember to find it in your heart to have faith in God again.

Trusting God looks nothing unusual but truly, it feels so calming and peaceful even amidst all the chaos that it feels purely magical.

Trusting God may feel resistive at times but once you have learned to leave it all in the hands of God, resistance will never knock on your doors.

Stuck in a situation?

Tell God, “I leave it in your hands. Do what is best for all.”

And see the magic.

Don’t fret. Don’t be uptight. Don’t worry about what God is doing. He knows the future better than we do.

Sometimes, trying hard ruins things. Hence, we need to loosen ourselves and convince our mind, heart, and soul that God’s got our back and He will make a way through the situations we cannot control.

I have experienced it endless times and say this from my experience, God does not like to let us down. God is just a call, a prayer, the faith of the size of a sand-grain away.

God is in your heart and He can solve all the problems without your having to force any certain outcomes.

God works in ways we cannot understand and that’s why we call His workings miracles.

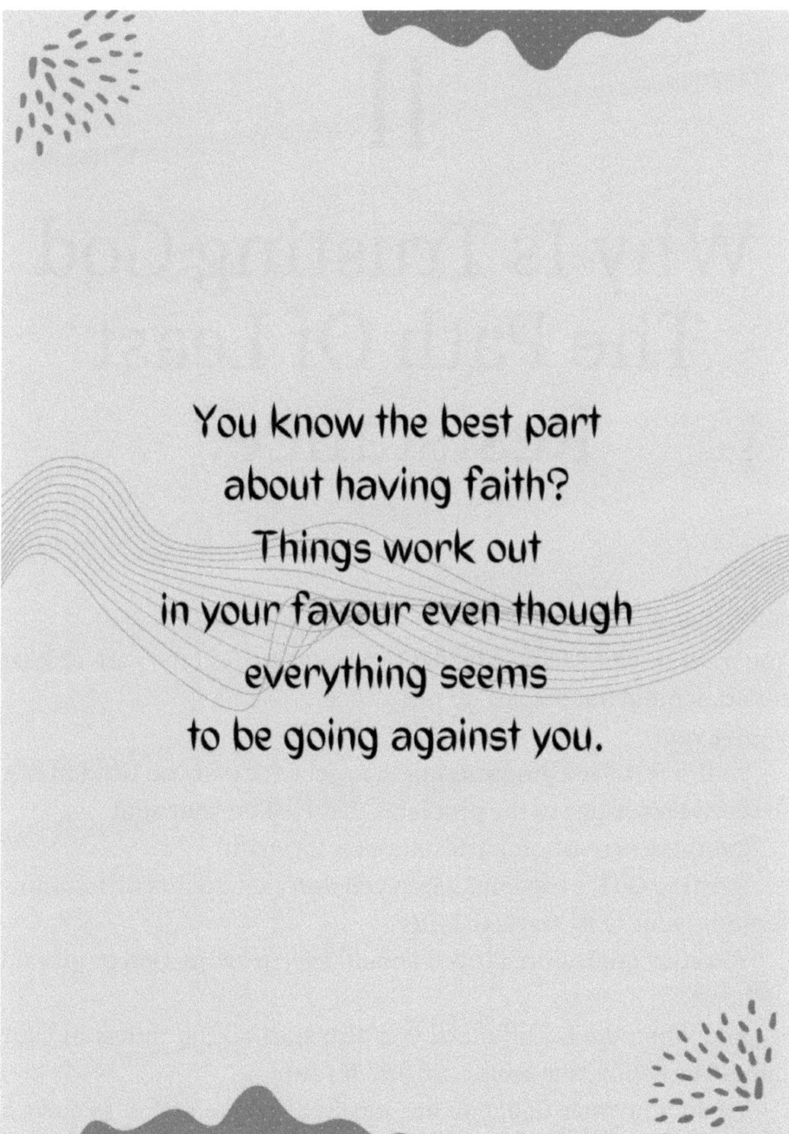
You know the best part
about having faith?
Things work out
in your favour even though
everything seems
to be going against you.

II

Why Is Trusting God The Path Of Least Resistance?

You must be wondering why did I call trusting God the path of least resistance and not zero or no resistance.

Are you?

Well, it is indeed the easiest path to get whatever you want in life, to receive solutions to the problems that feed on your soul.

But there sure is some resistance on this path.

Trusting God is easy but when you don't see results or solutions for long, your trust starts to falter.

You start questioning if you should keep trusting God or give up on hope.

And when the faith falters, you also start taking things in your hand. The action that feels hard and forced.

When you trust God, you are inspired to take action to solve a problem. Those inspired actions feel effortless.

There is waiting on the path of leaving things in the hands of God because God does everything in His perfect and divine timing.

If you try to hurry up the process, you show a lack of trust and faith and this creates resistance in your mind.

Just think about it for a moment:

How would you feel if you get out of the situation you are currently stuck in?

Would you feel free after forgiving and letting go of the person that broke your heart?

Would you feel elated getting your dream job or client?

Would you feel wonderful seeing a loved one recovering from an illness?

What would you do when your desire manifests?

Thank God?

Then, why not start shifting your focus from your current circumstances to feeling how you would feel when your wish comes true?

Why not thank God for the desired future now and leave the rest in the hands of the Almighty?

We create resistance on our own through our thoughts and feelings.

Remember, God can hear even the most silent prayers.

I am a huge believer of the law of attraction which states that who we are is a result of our past thoughts and beliefs.

But I believe more in God.

God created the universe. The universe can make your negative thoughts and beliefs your reality but there have been so many times when God saved me from having things I badly wanted but could possibly harm me in the future.

Here's an example from my life that I still cannot believe is my reality. It also shows what being a vibrational match to your future feels like. Being a vibrational match means tuning in to the feelings you would feel when your desire becomes your reality.

When my parents were looking for a match for me, I was not prepared for the wedding. I didn't want to marry a stranger but arranged marriage was chosen by God for me.

I always dreamt of marrying someone who loved me. People often wish to marry someone they love but I wanted a man who already loved and valued me.

Who could it be? I had no clue.

I still wasn't ready for marriage but my parents were adamant to get me married by a certain age.

One day, I was sitting with my mom and talking and after a while, a thought struck my mind: how badly I'd miss these moments after my marriage.

This became a recurring thought and guess what? Within a few weeks, I got engaged! He was a stranger but in our first meeting, his vibes just clicked and I readily agreed to marry him.

Also, he was someone who had fallen in love with me before we had even met or talked. He loved my photos, checked out my social media accounts, and was stubborn to meet me in person and obviously, he wanted to marry me only.

Whoever I met after the wedding from his side of the family told me the same story of how he had fallen for me.

God knew the perfect guy and the perfect way to bring us together.

Many people tried to drift our families apart with misunderstandings but all failed before his love and God's plans.

I didn't even know about his feelings until after a week of our engagement.

I was causing resistance on this part, too, because I didn't want to get married for the fear of an uncertain future.

At last, I left everything to God and said, "let your will be done. Whatever you have decided for me shall happen."

All that it took was letting go and letting God to meet the guy whom I proudly call my husband and I am now a part of the most loving, caring, and understanding family.

So, make it your mantra if you wish to deepen your faith and trust in God:

"Let Go and Let God"

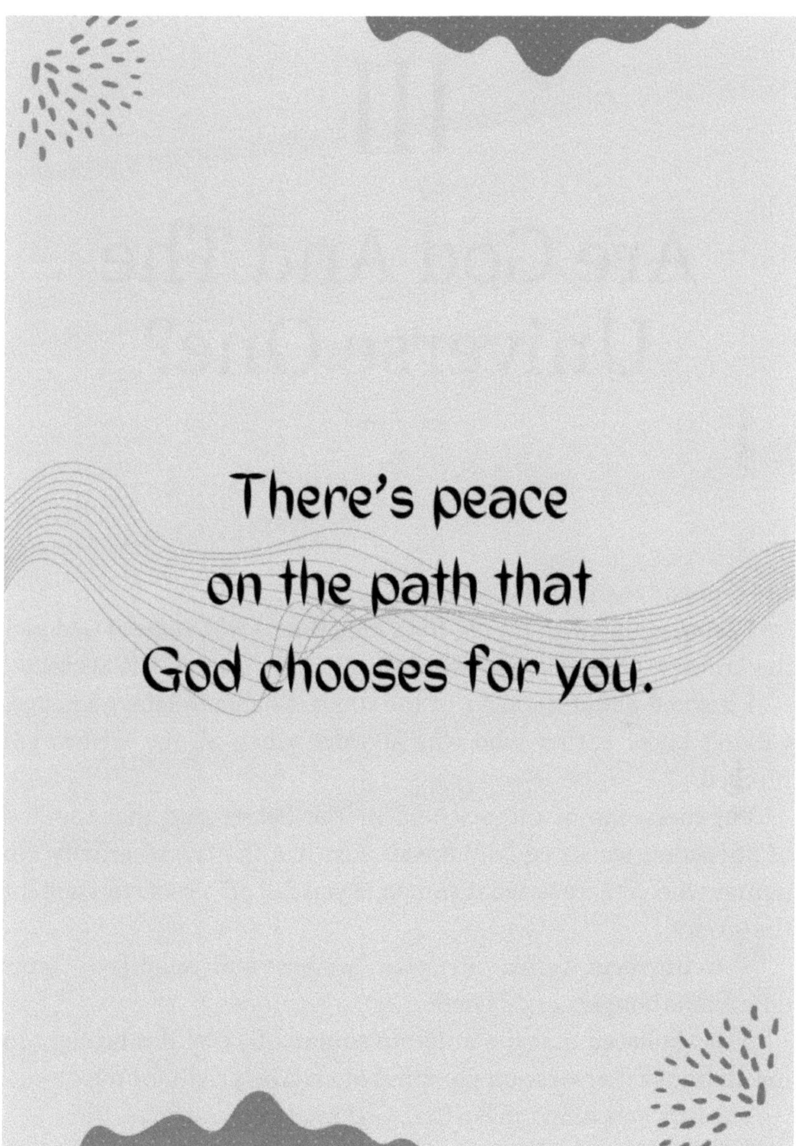
There's peace
on the path that
God chooses for you.

III

Are God And The Universe One?

Are God and the universe one?

I debated this with myself for a long time. I wondered if God and the universe are one or the same after I read the book The Secret.

I learned about the laws of the universe about eight years ago. I didn't know earlier who was at work when all my wishes got fulfilled.

But then, one of the teachers in The Secret said that the law of attraction works equally for all, just like the law of gravity. No matter who you are or what you do, if you fall off a roof, you will hit the ground.

The universe fulfils all your wishes and manifests your dominant thoughts and beliefs.

I also believed that the universe couldn't be God if it brought to me all things that were on my mind but weren't right for me.

The universe didn't make God. God made the universe.

What the universe can't do, God can.

And if the law of gravity makes you hit the ground after you fall, God can defy the law and catch you midway in His own ways and save you from the injury.

I hope you are getting my point here.

The laws can't fail but God is surely above all the laws and can alter the results of the laws on you.

I believe in the law of attraction and the universe but I believe and rely so much more on God.

I know that if the universe is about to manifest something in my life that I want but isn't right for me, God will save me from that.

Here's a piece from my book Poetic Letters To God that describes it all:

Dear God,
Thank you for giving me
everything that I ever
~~wanted~~ needed in my life
and saving me from what
wasn't meant to be mine.

Enter Caption

The debate if they are the same came to an end some time ago when an Instagram post's caption said: Universe is the *symphony*, God is the *composer*.

I don't know what else can describe the relationship of God and the universe better than this one sentence.

Coming back to if God and the universe are one, I believe that God is one with each and every one of His creations.

If you look at the mantra 'Shivoham', it is made from two words: Shiva+Aham. *Shiva* is for Lord Shiva and *Aham* is a Sanskrit word that means 'I am'.

So, Shivoham means 'I am Shiva'. The mantra reminds us of our oneness with our Creator, the ultimate truth.

The universe and God are one but they are not the same. God created the universe and the universe works according to the laws while God is above all—The Highest Power that there is.

If you don't believe in God and don't go well with the word God, just know Him as your ultimate creator.

The universe can manifest your not-so-optimistic thoughts even if your soul and intentions are pure but God will never do you wrong in that case.

In my opinion, an honest and pure heart is all that is required to call upon God and He will surely answer your every call.

At least, that's been my experience throughout my life.

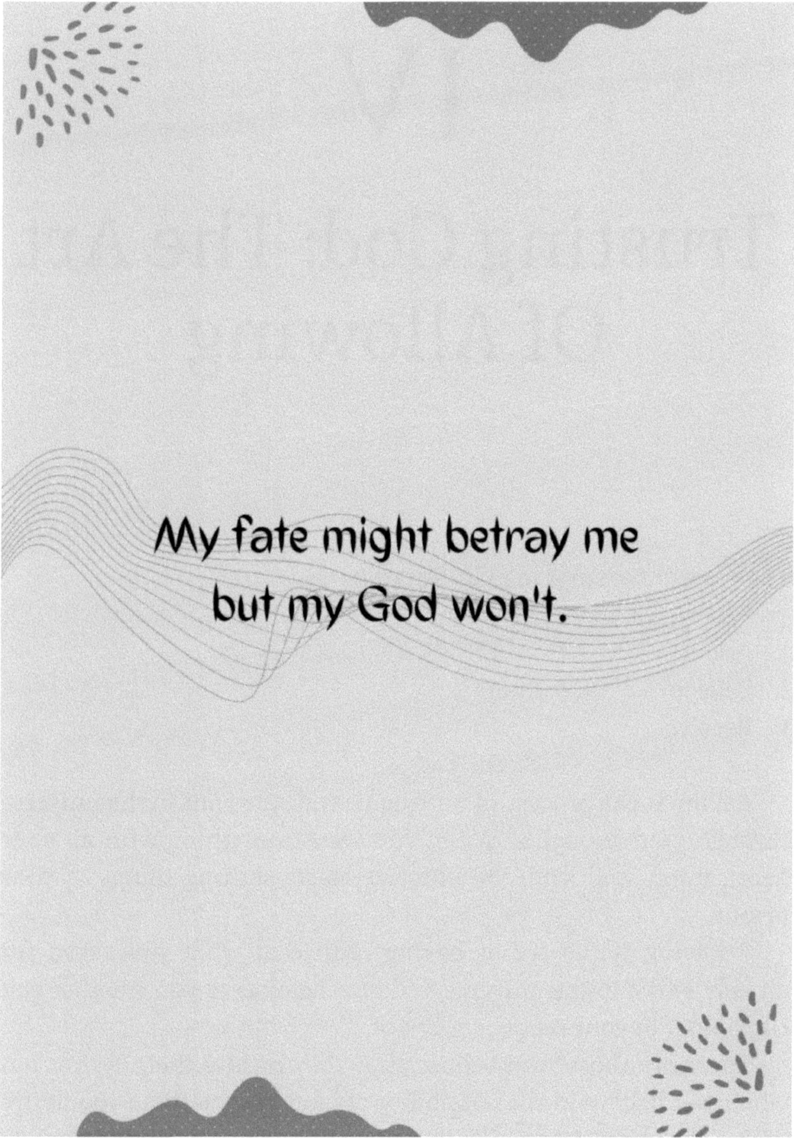
My fate might betray me
but my God won't.

IV

Trusting God: The Art Of Allowing

There are three steps to manifestation:

1. Ask
2. Believe
3. Receive

Asking is the process of putting your desires out in the universe through your thoughts. When you want something with all your heart, mind, and soul, the universe starts shifting things in your favour.

Believing is the act of having faith that what you asked for already exists in the universe and now belongs to you whether you can hold it in your reality yet or not.

There are those who believe after they receive their desires but when you believe in the possibility of having something you desire even before you see results in your reality, your wish is definitely going to be granted in the perfect timings.

The third step is receiving. Now, this is the step most of us get stuck on. We get so busy asking and *trying* to believe in the unseen that we get attached to the outcome of our desires.

We wish for things so desperately that we start sending out signals of lack, create a lot of resistance, and hence, start pushing our desires even farther away from us.

In my opinion, this is the toughest step of the manifestation; to allow ourselves to receive what the universe has to offer us.

And to allow ourselves to receive our fulfilled wishes, we need to learn to let go.

Surrendering to God puts you in the energy of receiving and cuts the chase. It allows you to let go and not worry about the outcome.

Letting go is tough at times and very easy at others. It depends on the kind of wishes you are making. When we are praying for others, there is less attachment to the wishes we are making as compared to when we want something desperately for ourselves. That's why prayers we make for others get fulfilled without us having to pray hard.

I had always struggled with letting go but only until I learned the art of trusting God.

I had to come to an understanding that we cannot control people and circumstances. We can only control how we respond to them.

There were times when I tried to convince people to make decisions that were convenient for me, when I tried to change circumstances with all my might but to no avail. I felt hopeless and powerless.

When nothing worked, I chose to let go and leave things in the hands of God. Trust me when I say this, there wasn't a time when God let me down. He never disappointed me. Even what seemed like a disappointment initially in some cases, turned out to be a blessing in disguise.

God knows our past, present, and even future. God has it all figured out. God has plans. God knows the perfect way out.

Gabriel Bernstein writes in her book The Universe Has Your Back: 'Your plans are in the way of God's plan.'

God has better plans than ours and we should, therefore, step back and let God lead our way, let God be our guide.

God has far better plans than we can ever imagine. We often ruin things when we try to manipulate people or circumstances to work out in our favour. The best way out is to trust that whatever God will decide and do will be for everyone's highest good.

Trusting God is the easiest way to practice the art of allowing and dissolving the resistance that our fears and doubts create on our path to receiving our desires.

'Let go and let God' has been one of my favourite mantras and it has never failed me.

Letting go fills your heart, mind, and soul with peace. It removes all blocks and lets whatever is for everyone's highest good to happen.

Trusting God is my sure-shot way to witness miracles continuously in my life. Trusting God helps me to let go of all attachments to my desired results and allow His will to be done.

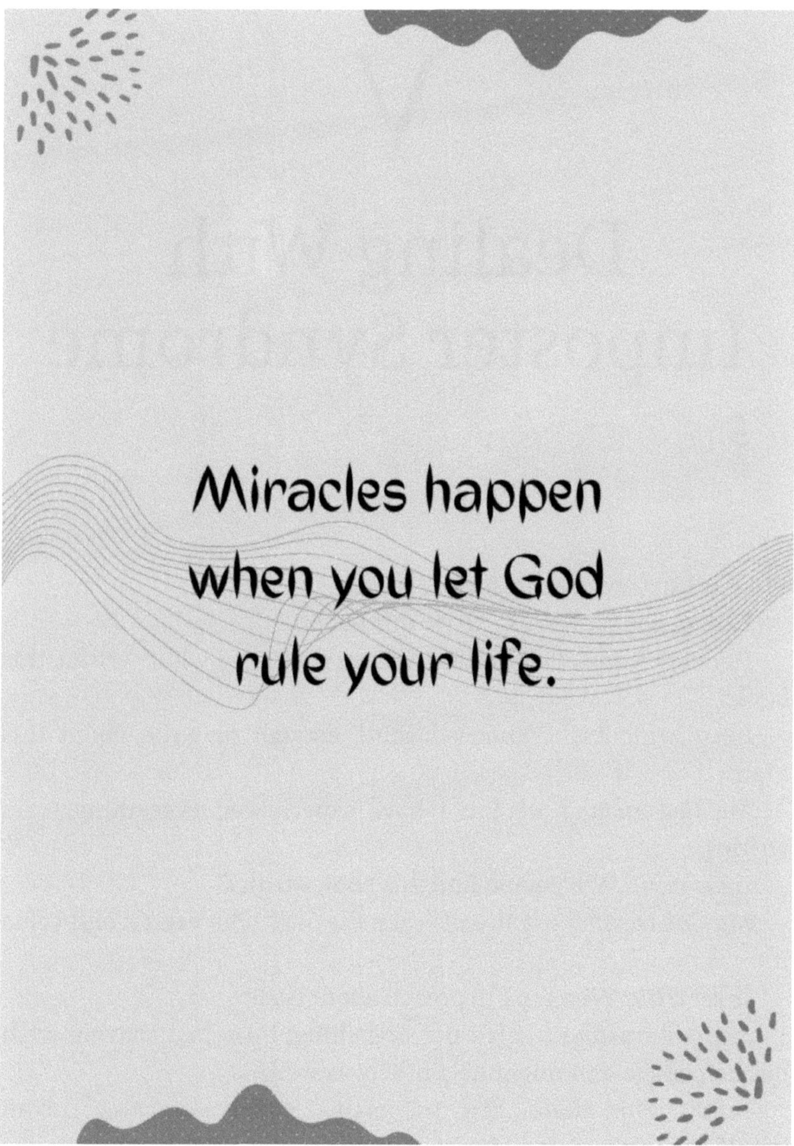
Miracles happen
when you let God
rule your life.

V

Dealing With Imposter Syndrome

What is imposter syndrome?

I am facing it even as I write this book.

Here are some of the inner conflicts that I had while writing this book:

Inner critic: Am I knowledgeable enough to write about this topic?

My God-trusting self: But I have experienced everything I am writing.

Inner critic: Will people find this book worthy?

My God-trusting self: It will reach the ones who need it and value it.

Inner critic: Who am I to preach about God?

My God-trusting self: It's not preaching, I am just sharing what has helped me and might help others as well.

Inner critic: There are so many people teaching about manifestation and the law of attraction, why do I need to do the same?

My God-trusting self: I am not teaching how to manifest but how to unstuck your manifestation stuck due to resistance.

Inner critic: Shouldn't you make this book free of cost?

My God-trusting self: A lot of hard work and time goes into writing, editing, and launching a book. I could put this energy into other tasks that pay instead. God gave me the idea to write this book so that I can also be benefitted from it through the price people pay to read it.

Does it sound familiar to you?

This is what imposter syndrome feels like.

Put in simple words, imposter syndrome is the terrible feeling that you get when you doubt your potential, your abilities, your skills, and feel like you are deceiving people with your work.

It's that thought of feeling not good enough.

I have had to let go of so many opportunities due to imposter syndrome.

I had faith in my first book Poetic Letters To God and hence, it performed well.

Though I knew that my second book The Book of Infinite Writing Prompts would serve people well, I had this nagging thought throughout its launch: *why would people love writing prompts as much as I do?* And, the book didn't do as well as I had anticipated.

You can see from the aforementioned dialogues that I am having a similar self-limiting conflict during this book as well.

The only reason that is keeping me going on the journey of writing this book is that God sent me this idea and I am bound to work on it anyhow, somehow.

I don't care how this book will perform, but it will reach those who would value it and be served by it.

I step back and let God write through me.

We are just a medium for God to express Himself. My ink, my hand, my paper, and my entire self are a way in which God channelises His messages and makes them reach the people who need to hear this.

I once accidentally stumbled upon the book The Golden Key by Emmet Fox and it was all that I needed to deal with all the tough situations in my life. The book was meant to reach me and so, it did.

If the author had decided to not put it out for the world, fearing the uncertain future, the book wouldn't have reached me or anyone else who benefited from it.

I now deal with imposter syndrome with these words:

'It's God who is working through me.'

God is using me as a medium to channelise His creativity, to make His message reach the world, and I trust God.

Here is one of the most quoted excerpts from the Shrimad Bhagwat Gita:

"Let your focus be on your action, let it not be on the outcome of the action. Do not act only out of expectation of a result, but then do not slip into inactivity." "2.47

One would argue that focusing on the outcome/results motivates them to take actions.

It's okay to know what outcome you desire but don't be so attached to it that your focus shifts from action to the outcome.

You do your work and leave the rest to God. When your intentions are pure, you receive everything that you deserve and more.

When working on anything, just think that God is working through you and you trust the actions that you are taking. The imposter syndrome will quickly find its way out the exit door.

Whenever I start convincing my mind that the tough task that I am doing is actually being done by God, I am left surprised with the amazing results.

God is the Highest Creator, if He can create this universe, this world, and you, why can't He create through you?

Think about it for a moment. If you believe that God can create through you, start calling Him to create through you every time you sit down to do a task and the imposter syndrome kicks in.

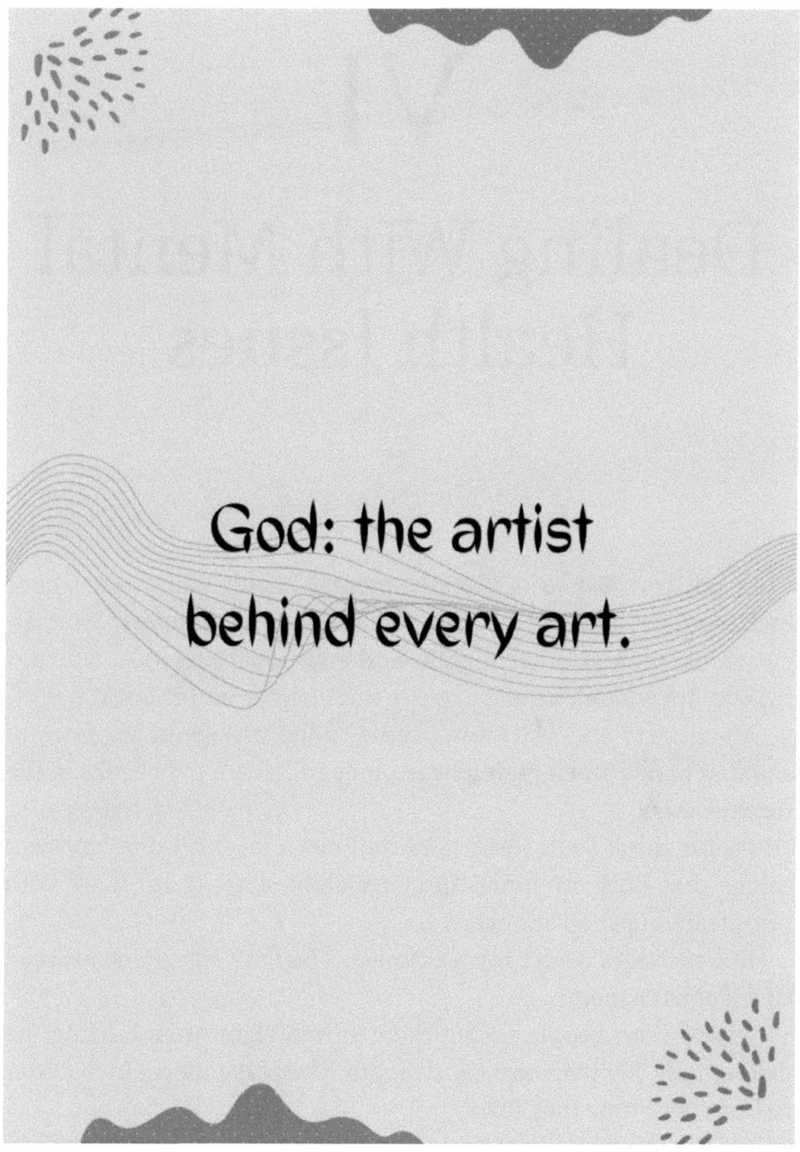
God: the artist
behind every art.

VI

Dealing With Mental Health Issues

I am not certified to talk about mental health issues but I have had my fair share of anxiety, body shaming, sadness, worries, overthinking, and other mental and emotional turmoils, which, I believe, are enough for me to write this chapter in this book.

My anxiety and fears don't come to the surface in the form of shaking hands and a racing heart, they roll down my cheeks in the form of tears.

People think I am weak because I cry a lot but I only cry over things that hurt my inner, insecure child, when I am filled with hurt, fear, anger, all at once.

But my tears aren't my weakness. They are my silent prayers, God listens to them.

I have seen people facing their karma right after hurting me deliberately. My tears are my strength. They take me an inch closer to God every time they flow.

During the times I cry, I want nothing more than to be left alone. In those moments, I won't no one by my side except God because I know that God doesn't want any justification or explanation for why my tears just won't stop coming, for why my heart feels heavy and pained.

I am anxious about meeting people, about new experiences, and sometimes about even stepping out of the home. Being an introvert, I cannot deal well with people and I always try to avoid meeting people who I am not comfortable with. But when I can no longer avoid the avoiding, I just have this option:

To trust God that everything will be alright

To step out and know that God is watching over me.

This has worked every time.

"Cast all your anxieties on Him, because He cares for you." -1 Peter 5:7

God will take care of your anxieties. God made you and you can't be anything less than perfect. God's creations cannot be imperfect.

God is guiding your journey, learn to recognise His messages and tiny miracles.

How many times did it happen that you lost balance and were about to fall flat on the floor but somehow did not?

Isn't it possible that God saved you just in time?

I quoted this example because it happened to me a million times and every time it happens, I make sure to thank God because who else would be saving me instead?

I am such an overthinker that there was a point in my life when I kept having imaginary negative conversations with negative people, which would totally exhaust me mentally.

When I could take no more, I decided that every time I talk to these people in my head, I will switch my conversations to God. I practised doing it a few times. I had imaginary conversations with God instead of those people. And within a few days, my habit of having negative conversations reduced to a significant extent.

I did not look up on Google for solutions, they came to me.

The answer to my every problem has been this: talk to God about your problem and let Him solve it.

Emmet Fox puts it the best in the book The Golden Key:

"If you are thinking about your difficulty, you are not thinking about God."

So, instead of thinking about what is bothering you, think about God. Who is God to you? What power do you believe in?

I love this quote by Seneca: "We suffer more in imagination than in reality."

It's so true in my case, at least. I have suffered so much in my head, to the point that I made myself cry by creating extraordinarily negative scenarios in my head. None of that ever came true. My reality has been far better than my negative imagination and thoughts.

What if we make our head the most peaceful place to reside in? That's where we spend most of our time, right?

And who can provide us more peace than God?

Fill your heart and head with the thoughts of God and see the magic yourself.

Disconnect from the negative to reconnect with God. These two cannot exist together, not even in your head.

Trust God. Make Him your best friend. Talk to Him and He shall answer in His own beautiful ways.

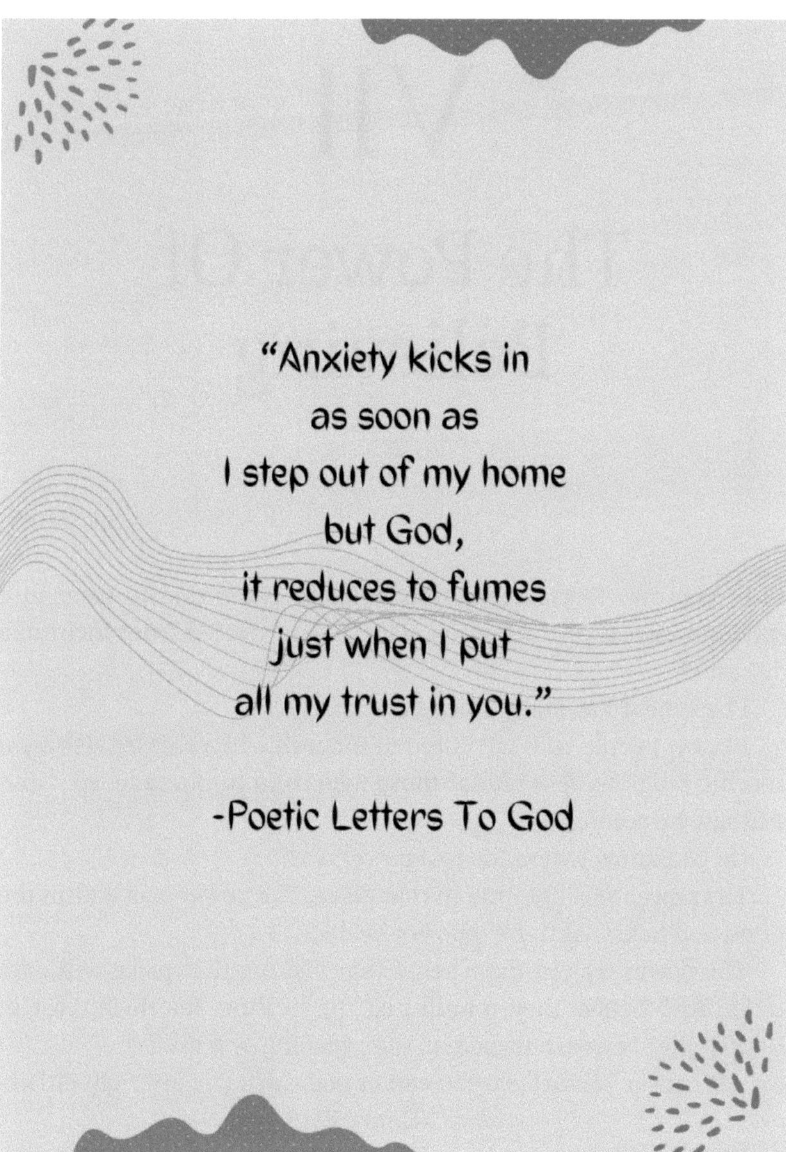
"Anxiety kicks in
as soon as
I step out of my home
but God,
it reduces to fumes
just when I put
all my trust in you."

-Poetic Letters To God

VII

The Power Of Believing

Have you ever heard the stories of those patients who went to a spiritual retreat or a religious place and recovered from incurable diseases?

I have heard so many stories of that kind.

I know people who got cured of incurable illnesses by visiting a specific religious spot and of those who went to the same spot and still saw no results.

Do you know where the real power was?

The power was not only in that place. The power was within the mind and hearts of those who got healed.

The power was in their belief that visiting that place will cure them. And hence, they manifested the healing. It's their trust in God/Higher Power that sped up their healing process.

"Whether you believe you can or you can't, you are right either way." -Henry Ford

Your beliefs create your reality. If you believe that you can be, do, or have whatever you want in life, nothing can ever block your way.

If you believe there is God in the temple, mosque, or church, you will always find God there. If you don't believe in God, these places might feel empty to you.

Even God wants nothing more than your faith and belief.

Prayers are hollow if they are not backed with belief.

And when you believe in what you pray for, God grants them for sure.

If you visit a temple with all your trust and faith that this place will heal you, you sure will be healed.

There is no such thing as incurable diseases. With the power of the mind, faith, and belief, you can defeat any disease, no matter how big or small. Our body knows how to heal itself. We just need to convince our mind of this belief.

My parents taught me early on in life, how to pray in such a way that I believe in what I pray for. That's the best thing that they ever did for me. They took me so close to God that they settled the rest of my life. Their teaching and my faith in God never ever failed me. It's been my saviour since ever.

My faith in God is unshakable. No matter what happens in my life, I know that God stands firmly by my side.

My real power lies in my belief in God and His divine grace.

You only find God in
the religious places
when He also resides
in Your heart.

VIII

Gratitude Is Not Overrated

Do you come across the word 'gratitude' and think how cliché and overrated it is?

What if I say gratitude is one step away from a totally different life?

I am boldly writing this because it definitely changed mine.

I started maintaining a gratitude journal in July 2015 after being inspired by The Secret, the book that directed me on the path of manifestation.

Since then, the wishes or dreams that I never thought were possible have come true every now and then.

If you wish to take one step towards a better life, just start gratitude journaling already.

Gratitude journaling is writing down a list of things that you are grateful for in your life. You may write it right after waking up in the morning or before going to sleep at night, or honestly, at any time of the day.

Even on the worst days, we have a lot to be grateful for. It can be as simple yet as important as the air we breathe and the food we eat or the roof that we have over our head.

Gratitude also sends out signals of trust and faith.

When you are grateful for the things that you want but don't have yet and feel thankful with all your heart, nothing can stop it from coming to you at the right time.

But it should be noted that you cannot fool God/universe with statements like, "thank you, God, for this and that." Words only have powers when they are backed with feelings. You have to be really grateful, ignoring the current reality which tells you that your desire isn't manifested yet.

Gratitude is the other form of believing. You cannot be grateful for the wishes yet to be fulfilled until you believe that what you want is already yours.

You must be wondering how can you feel grateful when you can clearly see that your wish is not fulfilled yet.

And the answer is faith. With faith the size of a mustard seed, you can move mountains.

Faith is the easiest to develop when you trust God and His intentions; when you believe in God's goodness, greatness, and ability.

The correct prayer is not a prayer in which we ask for certain things or wishes. A true prayer is when we thank God for things that we have and for those that we want.

Feeling gratitude fills our hearts with joy and peace, the highest frequency of emotions required to manifest anything that you ever want in life.

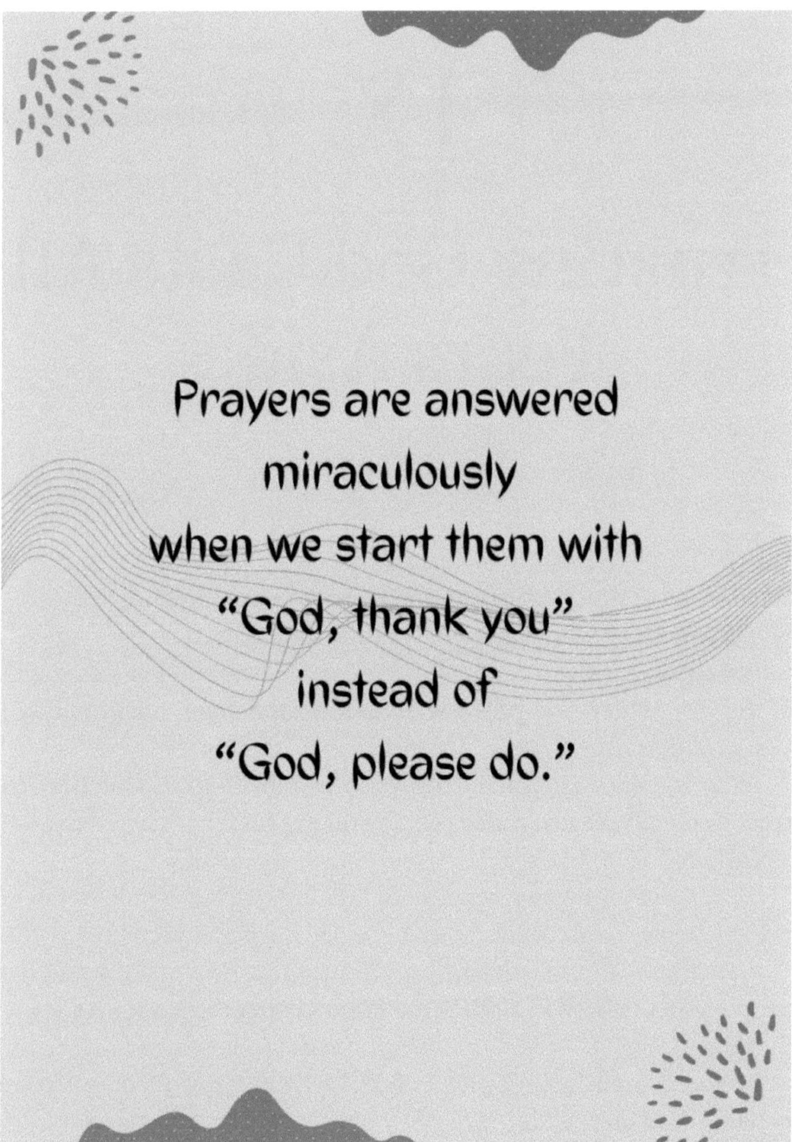
Prayers are answered
miraculously
when we start them with
"God, thank you"
instead of
"God, please do."

IX

Trusting God Casts All Fears Aside

Here is one of my favourite quotes from A Course In Miracles:

"If you knew who walked beside you, fear would be impossible."

If you simply just imagine God walking beside you at every step of the way (which God sure does, I believe), the mere thought makes you a million times braver, doesn't it?

Why is it easy for you to trust people and situations and hard to trust God who created those people and has total control over those situations?

If we did not have science today, everything would seem a miracle to us. Think about it, isn't science itself a miracle?

Some people don't believe in science and just that way, some people don't believe in God. Some others believe in both, and some in none.

If you can put your belief in fears, why can't you just put your belief in God instead?

After all, both are unseen by our eyes but felt by our hearts.

God doesn't make mistakes, humans do, yet you somehow find it easier to trust people over God.

But God is generous enough to help you through the people you place your trust in.

"I sought the Lord, and He heard me, and delivered me from all my fears." -PSALM 34:4

Ultimately, all the help, all the resources come to us from God.

Moreover, you don't need anyone to have a connection with God, no middleman is required. Just close your eyes and you will find God by your side.

Trusting God casts out all the fears from your life and fills it with peace and bliss.

"If you doubt God's intention – God's ability to produce the ultimate result — then how can you ever relax? How can you ever truly find peace?" -Conversations With God

Your wishes are answered far quicker when you relax and be at peace instead of restlessly and incessantly chasing your desires.

All our actions, at their deepest level, arise from one of these two emotions – fear or love.

When you put your fears to rest by placing your faith and trust in God, you fill all your heart with pure love.

And every action taken from a place of love will feel effortless, fun, inspired, and blessed.

Also, I have noticed that some religions or people fear God so much that they instil false beliefs of fear of God in people. Please, folks, if God won't be there for you, who else will be?

Why would God hurt you for messing up? God loves you more than anyone else in this world. Always look at God as your best friend and not someone you should be so afraid of that you stop believing in them. God has got you. God is the greatest friend you can ever have in your life.

I never let anyone's beliefs about fearing God come in my way of how I consider God my best friend, my saviour, my everything.

My parents never made me follow a certain God, or follow certain rules when it came to my relationship with God. They taught me the way I 'could' pray if I wanted to and not that I 'must' pray the way they taught me. Their this openness made me explore who God is to me and how I wish to stay connected to God.

The only time I fear God is when I am either lying or doing something that may potentially harm someone or something.

Else, nothing and nobody can make me fear the One who has stood by me no matter how many times I followed seemingly wrong paths.

As long as your intentions are pure, nothing can come between you and God.

So, take a backseat, know that what you want will come to you in God's perfect timing. Trust God, thank God, and let God enjoy the process of fulfilling your wishes and prayers. Don't push it away with the fear of not receiving the answers to your prayers in your desired timings.

And never fear God when you mess up because God forgives right at the moment you ask for forgiveness. Sometimes, we are more wrong in our own or people's eyes than we are in God's eyes. God forgives us like our parents do when we do something wrong.

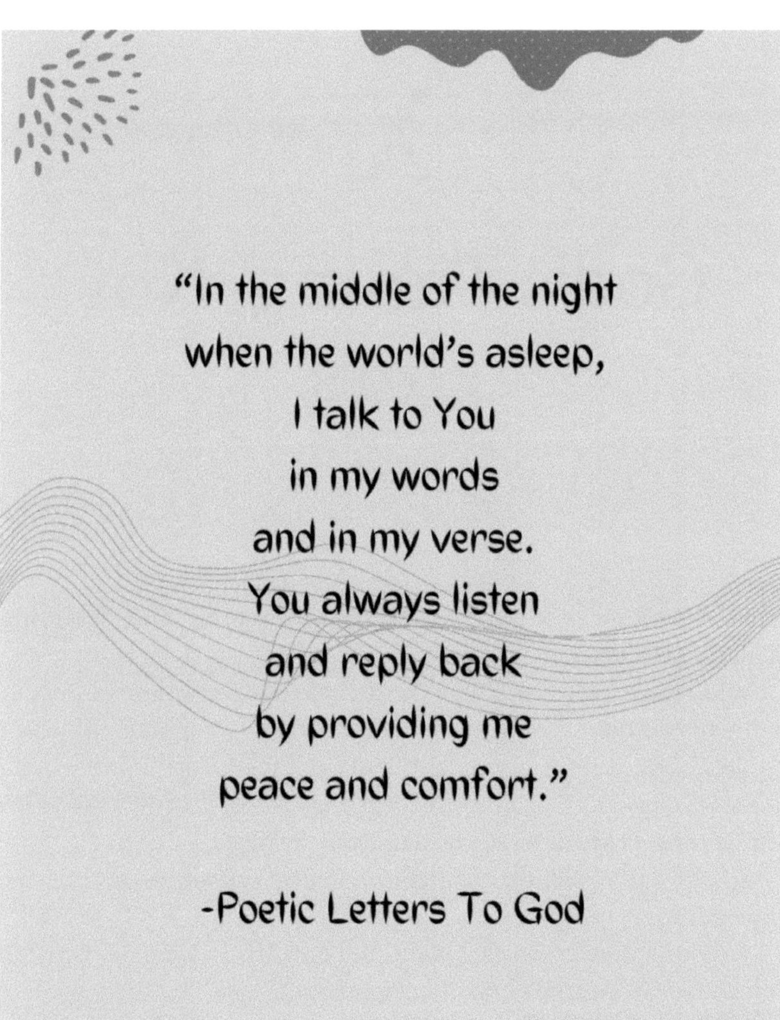
"In the middle of the night
when the world's asleep,
I talk to You
in my words
and in my verse.
You always listen
and reply back
by providing me
peace and comfort."

-Poetic Letters To God

X

God's Timing, Not Ours

Learn to wait on God. God has waited on you to become deserving of all that He has in store for you.

What is meant for you won't be delivered to any other address. It is already yours.

Think about it for a moment. You can't just teleport from India to the USA by deciding that you wish to go there. There's a whole lot of planning, preparations, and a journey involved.

You love the journey, don't you? Sometimes even more than the destination.

Wouldn't life be boring if you could have everything delivered to you while you sit all day long on your couch?

Ups and downs add interest in life. We won't value happy days if we don't know what sadness feels like.

God doesn't push us through troubled waters. He holds our hand and walks us through it. We just can't recognise His presence at times.

God shapes us into who we are meant to be.

Everything is a process. Take cooking, for example. You cannot eat raw ingredients, therefore you combine and cook them. You cannot eat sizzling hot food because you will burn your tongue with it, so, you let it come down to a certain temperature. Just like that, waiting on God means letting God prepare the right circumstances and conditions before He fulfils your wishes so that you are ready to receive them.

Just the way you enjoy your journey or certain processes in life, there is perfection in God's processes and ups and downs are a part of it.

Maybe God, too, wants to enjoy His journey with you.

Let God take His time and when the time is right, God will bless you with more than you can ever contain in your life.

If you ever wonder that God is not answering your prayers because God doesn't like your desires then you are wrong. God Himself placed the desire in your heart and He wants you to have whatever it is that you want but now may not be the right time.

You want something in your life because you are meant to have it. It's your fears of not having it or the lack of possibility of having it that just keep pushing it away from you.

The day you believe that you will have what you want is the day it starts coming to you. Don't go out looking for it and worry that it has not shown up yet. Sit back, relax, and know that the lesser you wait for it, the faster it arrives.

Nobody achieves overnight success (maybe, except a few) but people don't give up on their work just because they didn't see the results in one day. They work and let time do its job on the side. When they have full faith in their efforts, in their work, and believe that they will succeed one day, success comes to them when they are ready for it.

Trust God. Trust His timing. Trust the process.
God's timing, not ours.
God's plans, not ours.
God's will, not ours.

If God had given me all the things I wanted, I'd be in huge trouble today. His plans were better.

My plans/wishes were for only my good, His involved the good of everyone involved.

If God had given me certain things earlier than He did, I'd be cursing my fate today. His timings were perfect.

It's taken me years and a hell lot of experiences to understand that trusting God is my way out of every situation in my life.

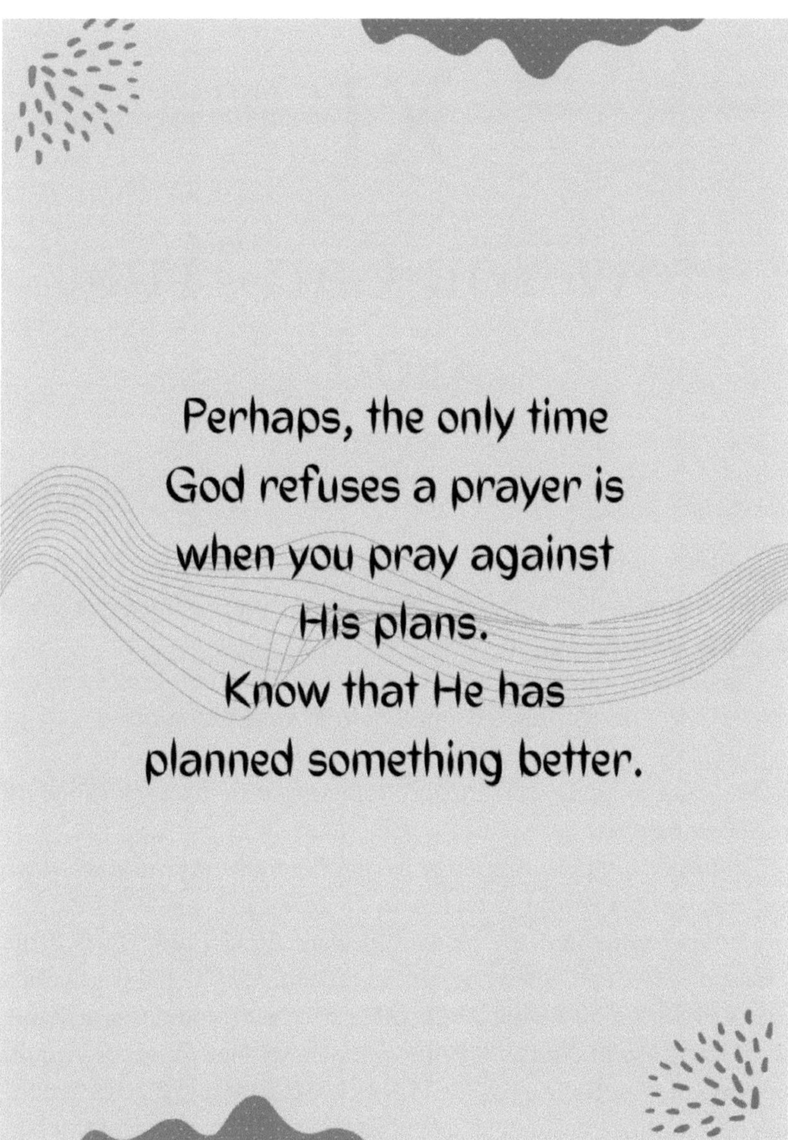
Perhaps, the only time
God refuses a prayer is
when you pray against
His plans.
Know that He has
planned something better.

XI

How You Can Trust God

As we step into the final and the longest chapter of this book, I feel weird to write it.

It isn't even the most important chapter because we all have our own ways of developing trust in God or anyone or anything

Who am I to tell you how you can trust God? No one. I am a fellow human being who trusted God ever since my parents taught me how to pray.

Honestly, my faith deepened in God the most in June 2008 when we met with a brutal accident in Dehradun. I, my brother, and my cousin with my uncle's family were on our way back from Mussoorie to Delhi when our car fell off a bridge or a hill (I still don't know. I was unconscious). The most unfortunate about this accident was losing our uncle and leaving our aunt with a spinal cord injury because of which she could no longer walk. That one day turned the life of our joint family upside down. It was the worst day of our life.

But, the least injured person in the accident was the person telling you about the incident. I was 13 years old. My mom had lost any hope of having her kids back home as soon as she heard the news.

Some weeks later, she told me one day, "perhaps, this saved you," pointing at the pendant of Mata Vaishno Devi around my neck which I was also wearing on that fateful day. I believed my mom. And my faith deepened in Her and Her pendant ever since.

I learned about the law of attraction and manifestation first in 2014, but I always believed a lot more in God.

Sure, manifestation works, but I also feel that God has saved me from many of my wishes that the universe could manifest but those fulfilled wishes could harm me later.

I don't know how your trust in God will develop but here are some ways that help me to connect with God or manifest my desires easily. They are tried and tested and not some stuff I just learned and put here in my words without experiencing.

SURRENDERING

Surrendering is the key to trusting God. It's like taking a leap of faith.

A baby smiles and laughs when thrown up in the air by their parent because they know that their parent will catch them and they won't fall.

God is your parent. You are God's child. How can God let you fall when you take a leap of faith?

It will hurt God more to see you fall than it would hurt you.

Surrendering rids you of fears and makes you feel powerful and peaceful.

You must have heard a thousand times or more 'the power is within you' and yet you often feel powerless.

I believe that the power within us is nothing more than our willingness to trust God... trust enough to help us and guide us through the situation.

When we fail to believe in ourselves, we start feeling restless and hopeless. That's when believing in God becomes mandatory, believing in some power higher than all of us.

To believe in God, all you have to do is surrender to God's will.

An example of surrendering comes again from the accident that I mentioned earlier. I don't remember much from that day but whatever I remember, I remember vividly. When our car was about to fall, I felt it bending to one side and rising up in the air from the other. I thought, "we are gone." I put my head down in my lap and considered it the end.

It still gives me goosebumps to think about it. It sounds like a nightmare but no matter how much we wish it was a nightmare, it was sadly our reality. I knew we could do nothing at that moment, but somehow, God saved 7 out of the 8 of us. But God also took away the most precious gem of our family that day. Maybe God, too, wants angels to be around him and not on this earth.

Here's one of the poems that I wrote for a collaboration wherein I wrote six poems for when your faith in God seems lost:

Tell me
why won't I
believe in God
when He brought me home,
just mildly injured
from a near-death experience,
back to my mom
who had lost all hopes.

Believing is your only way to develop trust in God. And to believe in God, you need to learn how to surrender to His will.

ꕤ

In this chapter, I have mentioned some of the ways in which you can surrender and leave your worries in the hands of God. Worrying is the worst use of your time and energy. So, why not choose peace instead?

Ways To Surrender

1. FOCUS ON GOD

Many people would call it meditation but I'll come to that in the next point. When I mentioned in the book that my parents taught me early in life about how to pray, I didn't mean that they taught me to sit in a temple and chant (though they taught me that as well). But you can't have temples everywhere, at all times. You sure can have God with you at all times though.

They taught me that whenever you face any trouble or feel stuck, close your eyes and see Mata Vaishno Devi through your mind's eyes. Focus there, tell Her your worries and ask for a solution.

That day, they gave me the gift of a lifetime. The easiest way to communicate with God. This teaching has never failed me be it at home, classroom, shopping mall, in an exam hall, in hospitals, or any place. God has always been with me and contacting God is just a moment away.

I never had a problem imagining/visualising the view that's so deeply etched in my heart, mind, and soul. I instantly feel calm and relaxed as soon as She appears before my mind's eyes and blesses me. I always write God as He/Him but I worship God in the form of Her. It's not about pronouns, really. God is One.

Now, you don't have to form an image of God forcefully, especially if you don't believe in God. But if you don't believe in God, you wouldn't have spent your hard-earned money on this book and come this far reading it.

Anyway, if you cannot form an image of God, that's completely okay. Just imagine a ball of glowing light, of the colour of your choice, maybe umm, white? and let it send you blessings and take your worries away.

I didn't call it meditation because focusing on God takes only a few seconds and you don't need comfortable seating and/or a quiet place. You just need your heart and mind.

2. MEDITATION

I meditate on and off. I don't meditate regularly because I always have things to do on my mind and other distractions or I am just lazy.

But I do meditate on the pages every single day. We call it journaling.

Meditation, in its simplest form, is sitting in a quiet, comfy place and focusing on your breath. When your mind starts to wander, gently bring back your attention to your breath.

People say even meditating for five minutes works. I would say I agree with them from the experience of however many meditation sessions I had.

Meditation provides clarity, peace, and calm to your mind. It shifts your focus from fears and worries to love and bliss.

Love is the purest form of God. Love is the emotion that overpowers every other emotion. Love connects you to God the most.

3. LETTERS TO GOD

I told you that I meditate on the pages. I journal. I love putting pen to paper the most in the whole world.

There's something about this practice that makes me forget all my worries, all my fears, everything.

Because I love pen and notebooks so much, that love helps me form the deepest connection with God on the pages.

I have been writing letters to God for more than a decade now, even before I learned anything about the laws of the universe or letters to the universe.

God has mostly always heard me through those letters. Sure, a lot went unheard but that happened for my own good.

Writing letters to God is easy. Just grab a pen and a paper and tell God about everything that is troubling you the way you would tell your best friend.

Do you know what's the best part about letters to God? You don't need to write every single detail because God already knows everything, even more than you do. It just feels relieving to share all your worries with someone who does not judge you and also has the power to help you.

I also have a free workbook to help you start writing letters to God, in case you are wondering about what to write in your letters. You may check it out on www.shilpagoel.com

You may also thank God in advance for the things that you want in your letters.

Surrender on the pages, in your journals, and write letters to God.

4. AFFIRMATIONS

Affirmations are the things we say to ourselves consistently. Who are you talking to when you talk in your mind, isn't that yourself?

We spend most of our time with ourselves and the things that we tell ourselves matter the most.

Affirmations can be positive or negative. They are working whether you believe in their powers or not.

Our subconscious mind (the one that is connected to the powers higher than us) cannot differentiate between truth and lies. Society fed you so many lies all your life, you believed, and your subconscious mind brought them into your reality.

If you can tell your mind that you are poor/broke, you can also tell it that you are rich because abundance is your birthright. This conscious feeding of thoughts to your mind is called affirming.

Worrying is also a form of affirming–it's the process of impressing negative words, thoughts, and scenarios on your mind that eventually becomes your reality.

Why not use positive words and thoughts instead?

Why not switch 'I don't have enough money' to 'I know more than enough money is coming to me and God will provide me that'?

Easy, don't you think so?

I love affirmations given in the book The Golden Key because they are so simple yet so powerful. Here are they and all of them are my favourites:

- there is no power but God
- I am the child of God, filled and surrounded by the perfect peace of God.
- God is love
- God is guiding me now
- God is with me (the best and the simplest of all)

I love writing affirmations in my journal. I can't recite them. Writing gives me joy. You may recite affirmations in your mind or out loud or you can stand in front of a mirror and say affirmations to yourself in the mirror. If you love singing, you can even sing along affirmations to the tune of your favourite songs.

You may find affirmations for your situation on the internet or you may come up with your own affirmations.

My favourite ones that I write every day are: I am love; God loves me; I love God.

Alternatively, when we read, write, or recite affirmations, our conscious mind starts rejecting them and they take longer to reach our subconscious mind (where all the solutions to your problems exist). In such cases, you may listen to the subliminal.

A subliminal is a piece of instrumental music with hidden affirmations. The music keeps our conscious mind busy while the affirmations directly reach our subconscious mind so that the conscious mind cannot contradict them.

I didn't believe in subliminals earlier but they have been working well for me for a few months. I also read comments while listening to the subliminals on YouTube. Knowing and believing that 'it worked for others, and hence, it will work for me too' make them work even faster for me. After all, all the power lies in believing.

5. LOOK FOR THE GOOD

God won't throw any situation at you, one, without knowing its solution and two, without having anything in return in it for you.

"No one is sent by accident to anyone" -A Course In Miracles

God makes you go through any situation in order to shape you into who you are meant to be. God knows your way out of the situation but first, He lets you learn the lesson and become the person He wants you to be.

There's an easy way out of every situation that turns all the situations in my favour every time. It's called 'looking for the good'.

If, even in your worst times, you can look for a little good in the situations, you can easily bring your mind out of that negative state.

Hold on to that one good thought until you find another good thing about the situation.

Let's take my example here: on the days when I used to feel dull and grumpy for the decline in my Instagram following, I would soothe myself by saying that bots/unwanted followers were being automatically removed from my account. I prefer quality over quantity. I felt more successful at 20k followers than I did at 85k.

I kept choosing more positive thoughts like 'now I can focus on other things' or 'let's focus on monetising my skills rather than chasing followers.'

And the result? I earned a lot more than I did in all my years by shifting my focus to freelancing, switching from Instagram to LinkedIn, easily grabbing clients, and also working on my blog and books.

Trying to beat and impress Instagram's algorithm with static posts in the world of reels was eating up all my time and energy.

Rather than staying stuck in a situation, I turned it in my favour by choosing better-feeling thoughts and shifting my focus.

I looked for the 'good' in the bad and therefore, I got to spend my time doing what I love doing the most—writing and blogging.

You don't have to jump from the most negative thoughts to the best possible thoughts. You have to level up by choosing a thought that feels slightly better than the last and continue doing so until you reach the emotions of joy and fulfilment.

This practice may be slightly hard to do when you are feeling extremely negative. But knowing that God hides the good in every bad situation makes it possible to choose better thoughts.

6. READ UPLIFTING QUOTES/WORD OF GOD

I am a lover of quotes, especially if they are about God. They reassure me that God is with me at all times, that God's plans and timings are perfect, that God will never fail me, and the list goes on.

Do one thing today, hop on Instagram, open the list of accounts that you are following and then, unfollow all those sad quotes pages. They drain your emotions even more.

Do you look at a relatable sad post and feel relieved that you are not alone, someone's also been through it? No? You rather think that it is your story written by someone else coincidently and then, feel even more miserable.

Those sad and negative posts are doing you no good. Believe me. They are creating more of what you don't want in your life—sadness.

After you are done unfollowing, look for accounts that post uplifting/positive quotes or those that post words from scriptures.

Here is my favourite one of all time that I read on @relyonjesus's Instagram page:

"Leave it in the hands that created you."

You may also look up on Google or Pinterest and find words that speak to your soul, that help you trust God a little more.

7. CONFESS, APOLOGISE, AND FORGIVE

God is the greatest of all. God forgives all of our sins. If you think that God isn't listening to you just because you have sinned in the past, close your eyes and confess your sins to God, no matter how big or small they are.

Ask for God's forgiveness. God forgives easily and immediately. Don't hold yourself back from taking this crucial step.

On the other hand, learn to forgive as well. If someone has wronged you, let it be their karma. Don't hold grudge against them and hand over your hurt to God. Let God take care of the rest.

If you won't forgive those who hurt you, you will keep hurting yourself more. Forgiveness brings peace to your mind and soul. Peace helps you to get closer to God.

Remember, you holding grudge against someone harms you more than it harms them. Forgive and free yourself. Remove them from your mind. Your mind deserves flowers, not weeds. And you cannot remove weeds if you keep watering them with your thoughts. Forgiveness helps you to release them from your mind.

8. REFLECT ON THE PAST

This one is my favourite.

Whenever your faith starts to shake, pause for a moment, think back on time and recall all the incidences—big or small—when God had your back.

Remember the moments when God sent a ray of hope in the darkest of your times.

Collect pieces of evidence from the past of magic, of miracles.

You know there have been times when God either answered your prayers at the right time or you felt grateful for an unanswered prayer later on in your life.

I wanted to be a doctor. I attempted and failed several entrance tests. The last hope that I had diminished in October 2014 when we were on our way back home from Vaishno Devi, Katra.

My dad informed me about that lost hope as soon as he got off the phone. In that moment, I made the final decision because I was exhausted now, I didn't want to tread on the stressful path anymore.

I gave up that day.

I chose another path because subconsciously, I had already fallen in love with English Literature, the degree that I was pursuing on the side as I dropped years to attempt pre-medical tests.

I can't put in words how grateful I feel today for giving up that day. Connecting the dots backwards, I realise how one thing led to the other over all these years and brought me here.

God gives us the desires of our hearts, the things we truly want in life. My dream to become a doctor was the dream of my ego-self and not my higher self. All my mind wanted was to be a doctor but my heart was never ready to go on that path.

If I were a doctor today, I would not be writing this book. I would have been healing bodies and not minds and souls.

I really love what I do now. Writing is my love and will always be.

I just mentioned one phase of my life here but there are uncountable incidences when even my unanswered prayers were blessings in disguise, let's not even get started on answered prayers.

God has always had my back and He has your back, too. Just trust Him for once.

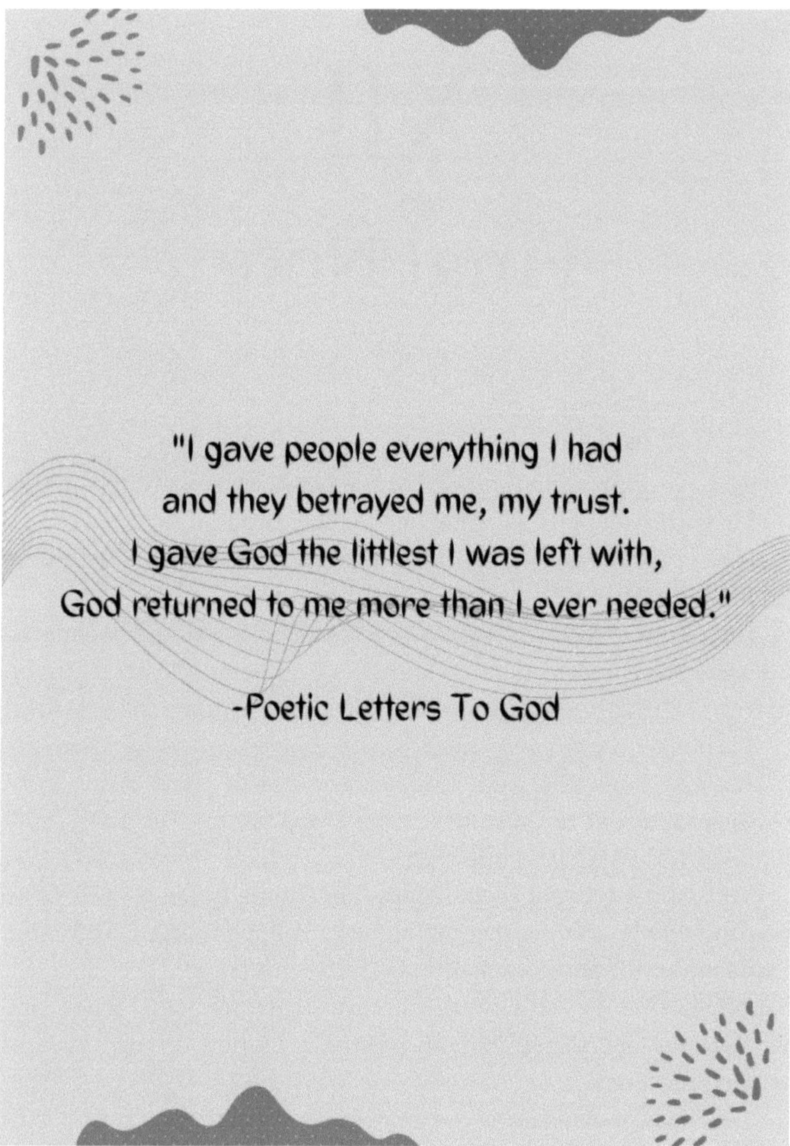
"I gave people everything I had
and they betrayed me, my trust.
I gave God the littlest I was left with,
God returned to me more than I ever needed."

-Poetic Letters To God

XII

Final Note

As we have approached the end of the book, I just want to say that God is within all of us. We only need to look within.

If we believe that a part of God exists within us, we would be invincible. God can do anything and so can we.

It took me years to write my previous books and the books that I have written and I am yet to launch. I completed the first draft on March 13, 2022. It took me less than 15 days to prepare the first draft of this book, do you know why?

Because I believed that God wanted me to write it urgently; because God sent me this idea while I was praying; because it felt like God was writing through me.

This isn't my usual speed. Ideas don't come to me so quickly to pen the whole book within half a month but my mind and hand made me sit for hours each day and write this book!

When God is with you, you overcome all your flaws and weaknesses—perfectionism and procrastination in my case of writing this book.

This book is imperfect. You may find it flawed even after all the rounds of editing but only I know how just trusting God helped me beat these two monsters whom we call perfectionism and procrastination.

I don't know how well this book will sell but I do know that writing this book has been one of the purest, calmest, most divine, and best experiences of my life. It was thrilling and I feel exhilarated and I just don't feel like stopping.

I love this book already for so many reasons. For someone who deals with imposter syndrome on a daily basis, claiming love for this book means the world to me.

I thank God for bringing this book into existence through me.

I trust God that the book will reach everyone who needs it and will value it.

I trust God that this book has something great in store for me as well.

Thank you for staying with me till the end of this book. You are a blessing from God as well. A blessing for me as a writer and for my words.

9 798889 752769

Printed by Libri Plureos GmbH in Hamburg,
Germany